Millionaire by 20 from Real Estate Investment

By

J Cyril

© Copyright 2023 by PDT – All rights reserved. It is not legal to reproduce, duplicate, or transmit any part of this document in either electronic means or printed format. Recording of this publication is strictly prohibited.

Contents

Chapter 1: Introduction to Real Estate Investment

1.1   Understanding the Basics of Real Estate Investment

Real estate investment is a lucrative and exciting venture that offers individuals the opportunity to build wealth and achieve financial success. However, before diving into this field, it is crucial to understand the basics of real estate investment.

At its core, real estate investment involves purchasing properties with the intention of generating income or profiting from their appreciation over time.

There are various types of real estate investments, including residential properties, commercial properties, and land. Each type has its own unique characteristics and potential for returns.

One key aspect of real estate investment is understanding the concept of cash flow. Cash flow refers to the income generated by a

property after deducting all expenses such as mortgage payments, property taxes, insurance, and maintenance costs. Positive cash flow occurs when the
rental income exceeds the expenses, while negative cash flow indicates that expenses exceed rental income.

To make informed investment decisions, it is essential to conduct thorough research on market conditions and property values. This involves analyzing factors such as location, demographics, economic trends, and supply and demand dynamics. By understanding these factors, investors can identify areas with high growth potential and choose properties that align with their investment goals.

Moreover, real estate investors must also consider their risk tolerance and investment strategy. Some investors prefer short-term strategies such as flipping properties for quick profits, while others focus on long-term appreciation through rental income or development projects. It is important to assess personal goals and preferences to determine which strategy suits individual circumstances best.

For example, let's consider a young investor named Sarah who wants to start her real estate journey by purchasing a residential property in an up-and-coming neighborhood. Sarah conducts extensive research on market trends in her area of interest and identifies a neighborhood experiencing significant growth due to new infrastructure developments and an influx of young professionals.

Sarah decides to purchase a fixer-upper property at a discounted price and renovate it to increase its value. She then rents out the property, generating a positive cash flow that covers her expenses and provides her with additional income. Over time, as the neighborhood continues to grow, Sarah's property appreciates in value, allowing her to build equity and potentially sell it for a profit in the future.

1.2 Exploring the Benefits of Investing in Real Estate

Investing in real estate offers numerous benefits that make it an attractive option for individuals looking to grow their wealth. Let's explore some of these benefits in detail.

Firstly, real estate investment provides a reliable source of passive income. Rental properties can generate consistent cash flow, allowing investors to earn money while maintaining full-time jobs or pursuing other ventures. This passive income stream can provide financial stability and freedom, especially when multiple properties are owned.

Additionally, real estate investments offer potential tax advantages. The tax code allows investors to deduct various expenses related to owning and managing rental properties, such as mortgage interest payments, property taxes, insurance premiums, and maintenance costs. These deductions can significantly reduce taxable income and result in substantial savings for investors.

Moreover, real estate is a tangible asset that tends to appreciate over time. Unlike stocks or bonds that can be volatile and subject to market fluctuations, real estate generally experiences steady appreciation in value.

This appreciation allows investors to build equity and potentially sell properties at a profit in the future.

Furthermore, investing in real estate provides diversification within an investment portfolio. By allocating funds across different asset classes such as stocks, bonds, and real estate, investors can mitigate risk and protect their wealth from market volatility. Real estate investments have historically shown low correlation with other asset classes, making them an effective diversification tool.

For instance, let's consider an investor named John who has a well-diversified investment portfolio consisting of stocks and bonds. However, he realizes that his portfolio lacks exposure to tangible assets like real estate. John decides to invest a portion of his funds in a commercial property, which generates rental income and appreciates in value over time. This real estate investment provides John with diversification and reduces the overall risk of his portfolio.

1.2   Analyzing Market Trends and Statistics

To make informed investment decisions, it is crucial to analyze market trends and statistics in the real estate industry. By understanding these trends, investors can identify opportunities, assess risks, and maximize their returns.

One important aspect of analyzing market trends is studying supply and demand dynamics. Understanding the balance between the number of available properties (supply) and the number of potential buyers or renters (demand) is essential for predicting future price movements. When demand exceeds supply, prices tend to rise, creating favorable conditions for sellers or landlords. Conversely, when supply exceeds demand, prices may decline, providing opportunities for buyers or tenants.

Market trends also encompass factors such as population growth, economic indicators, and demographic shifts. For example, an area experiencing rapid population growth due to job opportunities or migration may present attractive investment prospects. Similarly, economic indicators like GDP growth rates and employment levels can provide insights into the overall health of a market.

Analyzing market statistics involves examining data related to property values, rental rates, vacancy rates, and historical performance. This data helps investors identify areas with high potential for appreciation or rental income. It also allows them to compare different markets and make informed decisions about where to allocate their capital.

For instance, let's consider an investor named Emily who wants to invest in residential properties in two different cities: City A and City B. Emily analyzes market statistics such as average home prices, rental rates, vacancy rates, and historical appreciation rates for both cities.

She discovers that City A has experienced consistent population growth over the past decade due to its thriving tech industry. As a result, property values have steadily increased by an average of 8% per year. Rental rates have also risen, providing attractive cash flow opportunities for investors.

On the other hand, Emily finds that City B has experienced stagnant population growth and declining property values over the same period. Rental rates are relatively low, and vacancy rates are high, indicating a less favorable market for real estate investment.

Based on her analysis of market trends and statistics, Emily decides to focus her investments in City A, where she believes there is greater potential for long-term appreciation and rental income.

In conclusion, understanding the basics of real estate investment is crucial for aspiring investors. It involves grasping concepts such as cash flow, conducting thorough research on market conditions, and determining personal risk tolerance and investment strategy.

Chapter 2: Understanding Market Trends for Successful Investments

2.1 Analyzing Current Market Conditions and Predicting Future Trends

Analyzing current market conditions is crucial for making informed investment decisions. By understanding the current state of the market, investors can identify trends and anticipate future changes, allowing them to position themselves strategically for maximum returns.

One important aspect of analyzing market conditions is studying supply and demand dynamics. This involves examining factors such as population growth, job opportunities, and infrastructure development in a particular area. For example, if a city is experiencing rapid population growth and an increase in job opportunities, it is likely that there will be a high demand for housing. This presents an opportunity for real estate investors to capitalize on this trend by investing in residential properties.

Another factor to consider when analyzing market conditions is the overall economic climate. Economic indicators such as GDP growth, inflation rates, and interest rates can provide valuable insights into the health of the economy and its impact on the real estate market. For instance, during periods of low interest rates, borrowing costs are reduced, making it more affordable for individuals to purchase homes or invest in commercial properties.

Furthermore, it is essential to analyze local market trends specific to the type of investment being considered. For example, if you are interested in investing in commercial real estate, you would need to examine factors such as vacancy rates, rental prices, and demand from businesses in that particular area. On the other hand, if your focus is on residential properties, factors like average home prices, rental yields, and neighborhood amenities become more relevant.

Predicting future trends requires a combination of research and intuition. While historical data can provide insights into past trends and patterns, it is also important to stay updated with current news and developments that may impact the market. For instance, changes in government policies or regulations can have a significant influence on real estate markets.

Additionally, keeping an eye on emerging technologies or industries can help identify potential investment opportunities. For example, the rise of remote work due to advancements in technology has led to increased demand for flexible office spaces and co-working environments. By recognizing this trend early on, investors can position themselves to benefit from the growing demand for these types of properties.

To illustrate the importance of analyzing current market conditions and predicting future trends, let's consider a real-world example. Suppose you are considering investing in a residential property in a city that is experiencing significant population growth due to the establishment of a new tech hub. By analyzing current market conditions, you discover that there is a shortage of housing options in the area, leading to high rental prices and low vacancy rates. Additionally, you predict that the demand for housing will continue to increase as more tech companies set up operations in the city.

Based on this analysis, you decide to invest in a residential property with the intention of renting it out. As predicted, the demand for housing continues to rise, allowing you to charge higher rental prices and achieve a steady stream of income. Furthermore, as more tech companies move into the area and create job opportunities, property values also appreciate over time. By accurately analyzing current market conditions and predicting future trends, you have successfully identified a lucrative investment opportunity.

2.2 Identifying Lucrative Investment Opportunities

Identifying lucrative investment opportunities requires careful research and analysis. It involves evaluating various factors such as market trends, financial indicators, and risk-reward ratios to determine which investments have the potential for high returns.

One approach to identifying lucrative investment opportunities is by conducting thorough market research. This involves studying different sectors or asset classes within the real estate market and identifying areas where there is strong demand or potential for growth. For example, if you observe that there is an increasing interest in sustainable living and eco-friendly buildings, investing in green real estate projects may present an attractive opportunity.

Furthermore, analyzing financial indicators can help assess whether an investment opportunity is financially viable. This includes evaluating metrics such as return on investment (ROI), cash flow projections, and net operating income (NOI). By comparing these financial indicators to industry benchmarks or historical data, investors can determine whether the potential returns justify the risks involved.

Another aspect to consider when identifying lucrative investment opportunities is risk management. Every investment carries a certain level of risk, and it is important to assess and mitigate these risks to protect your capital. This involves conducting due diligence on the property or project, assessing market conditions, and considering potential challenges or obstacles that may arise.

Additionally, diversification is a key strategy for identifying lucrative investment opportunities. By spreading investments across different asset classes or geographic locations, investors can reduce their exposure to any single investment and increase their chances of achieving consistent returns. For example, instead of investing solely in residential properties, diversifying into commercial real estate or even other industries like hospitality or healthcare can provide additional sources of income and potential growth.

To illustrate the process of identifying lucrative investment opportunities, let's consider an example. Suppose you are researching potential investments in a coastal city that has recently experienced a surge in tourism. After analyzing market trends and conducting financial analysis, you identify an opportunity to invest in vacation rental properties.

You discover that there is high demand for short-term rentals due to the influx of tourists visiting the city throughout the year. Additionally, by analyzing financial indicators such as occupancy rates and average rental prices in popular tourist areas, you determine that there is significant profit potential in this market.

To manage risks associated with vacation rentals, you conduct thorough due diligence on each property under consideration. You assess factors such as location, property condition, local regulations regarding short-term rentals, and competition from other vacation rental operators.

Based on your research and analysis, you decide to invest in several vacation rental properties strategically located near popular tourist attractions. As predicted, the demand for short-term rentals remains strong over time, allowing you to achieve high occupancy rates and generate substantial rental income. Furthermore, as the city continues to attract more tourists, property values appreciate, providing an opportunity for capital appreciation.

By identifying this lucrative investment opportunity through comprehensive research and analysis, you have successfully positioned yourself to benefit from the growing tourism industry in the coastal city.

In conclusion, analyzing current market conditions and predicting future trends is essential for successful investments. By understanding supply and demand dynamics, economic indicators, and local market trends, investors can make informed decisions about where to allocate their capital.

Additionally, identifying lucrative investment opportunities requires thorough research, financial analysis, risk management strategies, and diversification. By incorporating these practices into your investment approach, you can increase your chances of achieving financial success in the real estate market.

Chapter 3: Building a Successful Real Estate Portfolio

3.1 Step-by-Step Guidance on Building a Diverse Portfolio

Building a diverse real estate portfolio is crucial for long-term success and mitigating risk. A diverse portfolio allows investors to spread their investments across different types of properties, locations, and investment strategies. This section will provide step-by-step guidance on how to build a diverse real estate portfolio.

Step 1 - Define your investment goals: Before diving into real estate investing, it is essential to define your investment goals. Are you looking for short- term profits or long-term appreciation? Do you want to generate rental income or focus on flipping properties? Understanding your goals will help you make informed decisions throughout the process.

Step 2 - Research the market: Conduct thorough research on the real estate market to identify emerging trends and potential investment opportunities. Look for areas with strong economic growth, job opportunities, and favorable demographics. Analyze historical data and projections to assess the potential for property value appreciation.

Step 3 - Determine your budget: Assess your financial situation and determine how much capital you can allocate towards real estate investments.
Consider factors such as down payments, closing costs, renovation expenses, and ongoing maintenance costs. It is crucial to have a clear understanding of your budget before proceeding further.

Step 4 - Choose investment strategies: There are various investment strategies in real estate, including flipping properties, generating rental income, investing in commercial properties, or participating in real estate crowdfunding platforms. Evaluate each strategy based on your goals, risk tolerance, and available resources.

Step 5 - Identify target properties: Once you have defined your investment strategy, start identifying target properties that align with your goals. Consider factors such as location, property type (residential or commercial), condition of the property, potential rental income or resale value.

Step 6 - Conduct due diligence: Before making any purchase decisions, conduct thorough due diligence on the target properties. This includes inspecting the property for any structural issues, reviewing financial statements, analyzing rental income potential, and assessing the neighborhood's growth prospects.

Step 7 - Secure financing: Determine the most suitable financing option for your real estate investments. This could include traditional bank loans, private lenders, or partnerships. Ensure that you have a solid understanding of the terms and conditions of the financing arrangement before proceeding.

Step 8 - Purchase and manage properties: Once you have secured financing, proceed with purchasing the selected properties. Develop a comprehensive property management plan to ensure efficient operations and maximize returns. This includes finding reliable tenants (if applicable), maintaining the property, and addressing any issues promptly.

Step 9 - Monitor and adjust: Regularly monitor your portfolio's performance and make adjustments as necessary. Stay updated on market trends, rental rates, and property values to identify opportunities for improvement or diversification.

By following these step-by-step guidelines, you can build a diverse real estate portfolio that aligns with your investment goals and maximizes your chances of success. Remember that building a portfolio takes time and patience; it is essential to stay focused on your long-term objectives while adapting to changing market conditions.

3.2 Strategies for Flipping Properties and Generating Rental Income

Flipping properties and generating rental income are two popular strategies in real estate investing that can yield significant profits when executed correctly. In this section, we will explore these strategies in detail and provide insights into how to implement them effectively.

Flipping Properties: Flipping properties involves purchasing undervalued or distressed properties, renovating them, and selling them at a higher price within a relatively short period. Here are some key strategies for successful property flipping:

1. Identify undervalued properties: Look for properties that are priced below their market value due to factors such as foreclosure, neglect, or motivated sellers. Conduct thorough research on comparable sales in the area to determine if there is potential for profit after renovation costs.

2. Renovate strategically: Focus on renovations that add value to the property without overspending. Prioritize essential repairs and upgrades that appeal to potential buyers, such as kitchen and bathroom renovations, fresh paint, landscaping, and improving curb appeal.

3. Time your sale: Timing is crucial when flipping properties. Monitor market conditions and aim to sell when demand is high and inventory is low. This will increase your chances of selling quickly and at a higher price.

Generating Rental Income: Generating rental income involves purchasing properties with the intention of renting them out to tenants. Here are some strategies for successful rental income generation:

- Choose the right location: Location plays a significant role in rental income generation. Look for areas with high demand for rentals, such as proximity to universities, business districts, or popular tourist destinations. Consider factors like safety, amenities, and accessibility.

- Analyze rental market trends: Research the local rental market to determine average rental rates, vacancy rates, and tenant preferences. This information will help you set competitive rental prices and attract quality tenants.

- Screen tenants carefully: Implement a thorough tenant screening process to ensure you select reliable tenants who will pay rent on time and take care of the property. Conduct background checks, verify employment and income, and check references from previous landlords.

- Maintain the property: Regular maintenance is essential for attracting and retaining quality tenants. Respond promptly to repair requests, conduct regular inspections, and keep the property in good condition.

- Adjust rents periodically: Stay updated on market trends and adjust rents periodically based on factors such as inflation, demand-supply dynamics, or improvements made to the property.

By implementing these strategies effectively while considering market conditions and individual property characteristics, you can maximize profits from both flipping properties and generating rental income.

3.3 Long-Term Appreciation as an Investment Strategy

Long-term appreciation is an investment strategy that focuses on acquiring properties with the potential for significant value appreciation over an extended period. While it may not provide immediate cash flow like rental income or flipping properties, long-term appreciation can yield substantial returns over time. Here are some insights into implementing this strategy effectively:

- Identify growth areas: Look for areas with strong economic fundamentals and potential for future growth. Factors such as job opportunities, infrastructure development, population growth, and urbanization can contribute to long-term property value appreciation.

- Analyze historical data: Study historical property value trends in the target area to assess its long-term appreciation potential. Look for consistent growth patterns and consider factors that have contributed to past appreciation.

- Consider emerging markets: Emerging markets often present opportunities for significant property value appreciation due to rapid urbanization and economic development. However, they also come with higher risks, so thorough research and due diligence are crucial.

- Diversify your portfolio: To mitigate risk, consider diversifying your portfolio across different locations and property types. This will help you capitalize on various market conditions and reduce the impact of localized downturns.

- Be patient: Long-term appreciation is a strategy that requires patience and a long-term perspective. Property values may not increase rapidly in the short term, but over time, they can deliver substantial returns.

- Monitor market indicators: Stay updated on market indicators such as interest rates, employment rates, population growth, and infrastructure projects that can impact property values in the long run. Adjust your investment strategy accordingly based on these indicators.

- Leverage tax benefits: Take advantage of tax benefits associated with long-term real estate investments, such as depreciation deductions or 1031 exchanges (in the United States). Consult with a tax professional to understand how these benefits can optimize your investment returns.

Long-term appreciation as an investment strategy requires careful analysis of market trends, patience, and a focus on acquiring properties with strong growth potential. By implementing this strategy alongside other investment strategies in your portfolio, you can create a balanced approach that maximizes both short-term profits and long-term wealth creation.

In conclusion, building a successful real estate portfolio requires careful planning, research, and execution. By following step-by-step guidance on building a diverse portfolio, implementing effective strategies for flipping properties and generating rental income, and considering long-term appreciation as an investment strategy, you can increase your chances of achieving financial success through real estate investment. Remember to adapt to changing market conditions, stay informed about industry trends, and continuously evaluate and adjust your portfolio to optimize returns. Start building your path towards becoming a millionaire today!

Chapter 4: Exploring Financing Options for Real Estate Investments

4.1 Understanding Different Financing Options Available to Investors

When it comes to real estate investments, understanding the different financing options available is crucial. Each option has its own advantages and disadvantages, and choosing the right one can greatly impact the success of your investment.

One common financing option is a traditional mortgage loan. This involves borrowing money from a bank or financial institution to purchase a property. The loan is secured by the property itself, and you make monthly payments over a fixed period of time. Traditional mortgages typically have lower interest rates compared to other financing options, making them an attractive choice for many investors.

Another financing option is private lending. This involves borrowing money from individuals or private companies instead of traditional lenders. Private lenders may be more flexible in their lending criteria and can provide faster approval times compared to banks. However, private lending often comes with higher interest rates and fees.

Investors can also consider using their own funds for financing their real estate investments. This could involve using personal savings or tapping into retirement accounts such as a self-directed IRA or 401(k). Using your own funds eliminates the need for borrowing and paying interest, but it also means tying up a significant amount of capital in one investment.

Additionally, there are creative financing options available such as seller financing or lease options. Seller financing occurs when the property owner acts as the lender and provides financing directly to the buyer. This can be beneficial for investors who may not qualify for traditional loans or want more flexibility in terms of repayment.

Lease options involve entering into an agreement where you have the option to purchase the property at a later date while renting it in the meantime. This allows investors to generate rental income while having time to secure traditional financing or improve their creditworthiness.

4.2 Evaluating the Pros and Cons of Each Financing Option

Each financing option comes with its own set of pros and cons, and it's important to carefully evaluate them before making a decision.

Traditional mortgage loans offer lower interest rates and longer repayment periods, making them a popular choice for many investors. They provide stability and predictability in terms of monthly payments, allowing investors to plan their finances accordingly. However, traditional mortgages often require a significant down payment and have strict qualification criteria, which may limit access for some investors.

Private lending can be a viable option for those who need quick financing or have difficulty qualifying for traditional loans. Private lenders may be more flexible in their lending criteria and can provide faster
approval times. However, private lending typically comes with higher interest rates and fees, which can significantly increase the cost of borrowing.

Using your own funds eliminates the need for borrowing and paying interest. It allows you to retain full control over your investment without relying on external lenders. However, tying up a large amount of capital in one investment can limit your ability to diversify or take advantage of other opportunities that may arise.

Seller financing provides an alternative option for investors who may not qualify for traditional loans or want more flexibility in terms of repayment. It allows buyers to negotiate favorable terms directly with the seller. However, seller financing may come with higher interest rates or require a larger down payment compared to traditional mortgages.

Lease options offer flexibility and time for investors to secure traditional financing or improve their creditworthiness while generating rental income. They allow investors to test the property before committing to purchase it. However, lease options may involve complex agreements and potential risks if the property value decreases during the lease period.

In conclusion, understanding the different financing options available is essential when investing in real estate. Each option has its own advantages and disadvantages that should be carefully evaluated based on your financial situation, investment goals, and risk tolerance. By considering these factors and conducting thorough research, you can make an informed decision that aligns with your investment strategy and maximizes your chances of success.

Chapter 5: Maximizing Tax Benefits in Real Estate Investment

5.1 Understanding Tax Deductions and Credits Related to Real Estate Investments

When it comes to real estate investments, understanding the tax deductions and credits available to you is crucial for maximizing your returns. These tax benefits can significantly reduce your overall tax liability and increase your cash flow. In this section, we will delve deeper into the various tax deductions and credits related to real estate investments, exploring areas not covered in the summary.

One of the most significant tax deductions available to real estate investors is depreciation. Depreciation allows you to deduct a portion of the cost of your investment property over its useful life. This deduction recognizes that properties deteriorate over time and lose value due to wear and tear. By claiming depreciation, you can offset your rental income and reduce your taxable income.

It's important to note that there are different methods for calculating depreciation, such as straight-line depreciation or accelerated depreciation using methods like MACRS (Modified Accelerated Cost Recovery System). Each method has its own advantages and considerations, so it's essential to consult with a tax professional who can help you determine the best approach for your specific situation.

Another valuable tax deduction related to real estate investments is mortgage interest. If you have taken out a loan to finance your investment property, you can deduct the interest paid on that loan from your taxable income. This deduction can be significant, especially in the early years of your mortgage when most of your payments go towards interest.

Additionally, expenses related to managing and maintaining your investment property are generally deductible. These expenses may include property management fees, repairs and maintenance costs, insurance premiums, advertising expenses for finding tenants, legal fees related to eviction proceedings or lease agreements, and even travel expenses incurred while visiting the property for business purposes.

Real estate investors may also be eligible for certain tax credits that directly reduce their tax liability dollar-for-dollar. One example is the Low- Income Housing Tax Credit (LIHTC), which incentivizes investors to provide affordable housing options. By investing in qualified low-income housing projects, investors can claim a credit equal to a percentage of their investment over a period of several years.

Another tax credit available to real estate investors is the Energy- Efficient Commercial Buildings Tax Deduction, also known as Section 179D. This credit encourages the construction or renovation of energy- efficient commercial buildings by providing deductions for eligible expenses related to energy-efficient systems and improvements.

It's important to stay updated on changes in tax laws and regulations that may impact your real estate investments. Tax laws are subject to change, and new incentives or deductions may be introduced while others expire. Consulting with a knowledgeable tax professional who specializes in real estate investments can help you navigate these complexities and ensure you are taking full advantage of all available tax benefits.

5.2 Strategies for Minimizing Tax Liability and Maximizing Returns

Minimizing tax liability and maximizing returns are key goals for any real estate investor. In this section, we will explore strategies that go beyond the basic understanding of tax benefits covered in the summary, providing new insights into how you can optimize your investments from a tax perspective.

One effective strategy for minimizing tax liability is through proper entity structuring. Choosing the right legal structure for your real estate investments can have significant tax implications. For example, forming a limited liability company (LLC) or a partnership can provide flexibility in allocating income and losses among multiple owners, potentially reducing overall taxes paid. On the other hand, operating as a sole proprietorship may limit certain deductions or credits available to you.

Another strategy is utilizing 1031 exchanges to defer capital gains taxes when selling an investment property. A 1031 exchange allows you to reinvest the proceeds from the sale into another like-kind property without recognizing capital gains immediately. By deferring taxes, you can keep more money working for you in the real estate market, potentially leading to higher returns over time.

Real estate investors can also take advantage of tax-advantaged retirement accounts, such as self-directed individual retirement accounts (IRAs) or solo 401(k)s. By investing in real estate through these accounts, you can enjoy tax-deferred or tax-free growth on your investments. This strategy allows you to build wealth while minimizing current tax liabilities.

Additionally, properly documenting and tracking expenses related to your real estate investments is crucial for maximizing deductions and minimizing tax liability. Maintaining organized records of all income and expenses, including receipts and invoices, will help ensure that you claim all eligible deductions accurately. Utilizing accounting software or hiring a professional bookkeeper can streamline this process and provide peace of mind during tax season.

Lastly, it's important to consider the timing of your real estate transactions strategically. By carefully planning when to buy or sell properties, you can optimize your tax position. For example, if you anticipate higher taxable income in a particular year, it may be beneficial to delay selling a property with significant capital gains until a year with lower income levels. Similarly, if you have losses from other investments or businesses, strategically timing the sale of a property with gains can offset those losses and reduce your overall tax liability.

In conclusion, understanding the various tax deductions and credits related to real estate investments is essential for maximizing returns. Depreciation, mortgage interest deductions, and deductible expenses are just a few examples of valuable deductions available to real estate investors. Additionally, exploring strategies such as entity structuring, 1031 exchanges, utilizing tax-advantaged retirement accounts, proper documentation and tracking of expenses, and strategic timing of transactions can further minimize tax liability and maximize returns. By implementing these strategies and staying informed about changes in tax laws and regulations, real estate investors can unlock the full potential of their investments while optimizing their financial outcomes.

Chapter 6: Managing Risks in Real Estate Investments

6.1 Identifying Potential Risks Associated with Real Estate Investments

Real estate investments can be highly lucrative, but they also come with their fair share of risks. It is crucial for investors to identify and understand these potential risks in order to make informed decisions and mitigate any negative impacts on their investments.

One of the primary risks associated with real estate investments is market volatility. The real estate market is subject to fluctuations, influenced by factors such as economic conditions, interest rates, and supply and demand dynamics. For example, during an economic downturn, property values may decline, leading to potential losses for investors. On the other hand, during a booming economy, property prices may skyrocket, creating opportunities for substantial profits.

Another risk that investors need to consider is liquidity risk. Real estate investments are typically illiquid assets, meaning they cannot be easily converted into cash without significant time and effort. Unlike stocks or bonds that can be sold quickly on the open market, selling a property can take months or even years. This lack of liquidity can pose challenges if an investor needs immediate access to funds or wants to exit an investment quickly.

Additionally, there are operational risks associated with real estate investments. These include issues such as tenant vacancies, property maintenance costs, and unexpected repairs. For instance, if a rental property remains vacant for an extended period of time, it can result in a loss of rental income and increased carrying costs for the investor. Similarly, unforeseen repairs or maintenance issues can eat into profitability and require additional capital investment.

Legal and regulatory risks are also important considerations when investing in real estate. Changes in zoning laws or building codes can impact the feasibility of a project or require costly modifications.
Additionally, disputes with tenants or legal liabilities related to property ownership can lead to financial losses and legal expenses.

To further illustrate these potential risks associated with real estate investments, let's consider a hypothetical scenario. Imagine an investor purchases a residential property with the intention of renting it out for passive income. Initially, everything seems to be going well, and the property is generating steady rental income. However, a sudden economic downturn leads to job losses in the area, resulting in a high vacancy rate and difficulty finding new tenants. The investor is now faced with the challenge of covering mortgage payments and other expenses without rental income, potentially leading to financial strain.

6.2 Implementing Risk Management Techniques to Ensure Profitability

While real estate investments come with inherent risks, there are several risk management techniques that investors can employ to ensure profitability and minimize potential losses.

Diversification is a key strategy in managing risk in real estate investments. By diversifying their portfolio across different types of properties or locations, investors can reduce their exposure to market volatility. For example, investing in both residential and commercial properties or spreading investments across different cities or regions can help mitigate the impact of localized market fluctuations.

Thorough due diligence is another crucial aspect of risk management in real estate investments. Before making any investment decisions, investors should conduct extensive research on the property's location, market trends, and potential risks specific to that area. This includes analyzing factors such as population growth, employment rates, infrastructure development plans, and local amenities. By thoroughly understanding the market dynamics and potential risks associated with a particular investment opportunity, investors can make more informed decisions.

Proper financial analysis is also essential for managing risks in real estate investments. Investors should carefully evaluate the financial viability of a project by considering factors such as cash flow projections, return on investment (ROI), and potential exit strategies. Conducting sensitivity analyses that account for various scenarios can help identify potential risks and assess their impact on profitability.

Risk mitigation strategies such as insurance coverage can provide additional protection for real estate investments. Property insurance policies can safeguard against damages caused by natural disasters or accidents while liability insurance can protect against legal claims. Investors should carefully review their insurance options and ensure they have adequate coverage to mitigate potential financial losses. Furthermore, maintaining a contingency fund is crucial for managing unexpected expenses and mitigating risks. Having a reserve of funds set aside specifically for unforeseen repairs, vacancies, or other emergencies can help investors navigate challenging situations without compromising profitability.

To illustrate the implementation of risk management techniques, let's consider an example. Suppose an investor owns a portfolio of rental properties in different cities. By diversifying their investments across multiple locations, they reduce the risk of being heavily impacted by localized economic downturns or market fluctuations. Additionally, the investor conducts thorough due diligence before acquiring each property, analyzing factors such as local employment rates and population growth to assess the long-term demand for rental properties in those areas. They also maintain a contingency fund to cover unexpected repairs or vacancies, ensuring that any unforeseen expenses do not significantly impact their overall profitability.

In conclusion, identifying potential risks associated with real estate investments is crucial for investors to make informed decisions and protect their investments. Market volatility, liquidity risk, operational challenges, and legal and regulatory risks are some of the key risks that need to be considered. However, by implementing risk management techniques such as diversification, thorough due diligence, financial analysis, insurance coverage, and maintaining contingency funds, investors can mitigate these risks and ensure profitability in their real estate investment.

Chapter 7: Motivation and Practical Advice for Young Investors

7.1: Inspiring Stories and Real-Life Examples of Young Millionaire Investors

In "Millionaire by 20 from Real Estate Investment," we aim to inspire and motivate young investors by sharing real-life examples of individuals who have achieved millionaire status through real estate investment at a young age. These stories serve as powerful reminders that financial success is attainable with the right mindset, strategies, and dedication.
One such inspiring story is that of Alex Rodriguez, who started investing in real estate at the age of 18.

Despite coming from a modest background, Rodriguez had a burning desire to create wealth for himself and his family. He began by purchasing a small fixer-upper property with his savings and spent months renovating it himself. Once the property was ready, he sold it for a significant profit.
This initial success fueled his passion for real estate investment, and he continued to buy, renovate, and sell properties throughout his college years. By the time he turned 25, Rodriguez had amassed a multi-million dollar real estate portfolio.

Rodriguez's story highlights the importance of starting early and taking calculated risks in real estate investment. It also emphasizes the value of hands-on experience and learning through practical application. While formal education can provide a solid foundation, nothing beats the lessons learned on the ground.

Another example is Sarah Johnson, who became a millionaire through rental income properties. Johnson recognized the potential in her local market for affordable housing rentals due to an influx of young professionals seeking accommodation. She purchased several properties near universities and colleges and converted them into rental units. By providing quality housing at competitive prices, she quickly built a reputation as a reliable landlord.

Johnson's success lies in her ability to identify emerging trends and capitalize on them. She understood the demand for affordable rentals among students and leveraged this knowledge to build her portfolio strategically. Her story demonstrates that being attuned to market needs can lead to substantial financial gains.

These real-life examples of young millionaire investors showcase the possibilities that exist in the world of real estate investment. They prove that age is not a barrier to success and that with determination, knowledge, and perseverance, anyone can achieve financial independence through real estate.

7.2: Igniting the Entrepreneurial Spirit and Empowering Financial Independence

In "Millionaire by 20 from Real Estate Investment," we not only aim to inspire young investors but also ignite their entrepreneurial spirit and empower them to attain financial independence. We believe that true wealth creation goes beyond simply accumulating money; it involves developing a mindset that fosters innovation, creativity, and a sense of purpose.

To ignite the entrepreneurial spirit, it is crucial to encourage young investors to think outside the box and challenge conventional wisdom. In the world of real estate investment, this means exploring alternative strategies and niches that may offer unique opportunities for growth. For example, instead of solely focusing on residential properties, aspiring investors could consider commercial or industrial properties, which often yield higher returns.

Empowering financial independence requires equipping young investors with the necessary knowledge and skills to make informed decisions. This includes understanding market trends, conducting thorough due diligence on potential investments, and developing effective risk management strategies. By providing practical advice on these topics in our book, we aim to empower readers to take control of their financial future.

Furthermore, we emphasize the importance of continuous learning and personal development. Successful entrepreneurs understand that staying ahead in an ever-evolving industry requires constant adaptation and improvement. We encourage young investors to seek out mentors or join networking groups where they can learn from experienced professionals in the field.

Financial independence also entails having a clear vision and setting achievable goals. We guide readers through the process of defining their objectives and creating actionable plans to reach them. By breaking down long-term goals into smaller milestones, young investors can track their progress and stay motivated along their journey.

Lastly, we stress the significance of perseverance and resilience. Building wealth through real estate investment is not without its challenges and setbacks. It requires patience, determination, and the ability to learn from failures. By sharing stories of successful investors who overcame obstacles, we aim to instill a sense of resilience in our readers.

In conclusion, "Millionaire by 20 from Real Estate Investment" goes beyond providing practical advice on real estate investment. It seeks to ignite the entrepreneurial spirit within young investors and empower them to achieve financial independence. Through inspiring stories, practical guidance, and a focus on personal development, we aim to equip readers with the tools they need to succeed in the world of real estate investment and beyond. So, if you are ready to embark on a journey towards financial freedom, let us be your guide as you build your path to becoming a millionaire!

Chapter 8: Conclusion - Your Path to Becoming a Millionaire

8.1 Recap of Key Takeaways from the Book

Throughout "Millionaire by 20 from Real Estate Investment," we have provided you with a wealth of information and insights to help you achieve financial success through real estate investment. Let's recap some of the key takeaways from this book:

1. Understanding Market Trends: One of the fundamental aspects of successful real estate investment is understanding market trends. By analyzing data and staying informed about local and national real estate markets, you can identify opportunities for growth and make informed investment decisions.

2. Identifying Lucrative Investment Opportunities: We have discussed various strategies for identifying lucrative investment opportunities, such as flipping properties, rental income, and long-term appreciation. Each strategy has its own advantages and considerations, so it's important to choose the one that aligns with your goals and resources.

3. Financing Options: Real estate investment often requires significant capital, but there are various financing options available to investors. From traditional bank loans to private lenders or partnerships, exploring different financing avenues can help you leverage your investments and maximize returns.

4. Tax Benefits: Real estate investment offers several tax benefits that can significantly impact your bottom line. Understanding these benefits, such as depreciation deductions or 1031 exchanges, can help you minimize tax liabilities and increase your overall profitability.

5. Risk Management Techniques: Investing in real estate comes with inherent risks, but there are strategies you can employ to mitigate those risks. Diversifying your portfolio, conducting thorough due diligence on properties, and having contingency plans in place are just a few examples of risk management techniques discussed in this book.

6. Continuous Learning: The world of real estate investment is constantly evolving, so it's crucial to stay updated on industry trends and best practices. Continuously educating yourself through books, seminars, networking events, or mentorship programs will ensure that you are equipped with the knowledge and skills needed to succeed.

By incorporating these key takeaways into your investment approach, you will be well on your way to building a successful real estate portfolio and achieving financial freedom.

8.2 Final Words of Encouragement and Next Steps in Your Journey

Congratulations! By reading "Millionaire by 20 from Real Estate Investment," you have taken the first step towards realizing your dreams of becoming a millionaire through real estate. As we conclude this book, we want to leave you with some final words of encouragement and guidance for the next steps in your journey.

Firstly, it's important to remember that success in real estate investment requires dedication, discipline, and perseverance. Building wealth through real estate is not an overnight process but rather a long-term commitment. Stay focused on your goals and maintain a positive mindset even during challenging times.

Next, continue expanding your knowledge and expertise in the field of real estate investment. While this book provides a solid foundation, there is always more to learn. Seek out additional resources such as industry publications, podcasts, or online courses that can further enhance your understanding of real estate markets, investment strategies, and financial management.

Networking is another crucial aspect of your journey towards becoming a millionaire through real estate. Surround yourself with like-minded individuals who share your passion for investing and can offer valuable insights or opportunities. Attend local real estate meetups or join online communities where you can connect with experienced investors who can mentor and guide you along the way.

As you progress in your journey, don't be afraid to take calculated risks. Real estate investment inherently involves some level of risk-taking, but by conducting thorough research and analysis, you can minimize potential pitfalls. Be open to exploring new markets or trying different investment strategies that align with your goals.

Lastly, always remember the importance of patience and persistence. Rome wasn't built in a day, and neither will your real estate empire. Stay committed to your long-term vision and be prepared to adapt and adjust your strategies as needed. Real estate investment is a dynamic field, and the ability to pivot when necessary is crucial for long-term success.

In conclusion, "Millionaire by 20 from Real Estate Investment" has provided you with the tools, knowledge, and inspiration to embark on your path towards financial freedom. By applying the key takeaways from this book, continuously learning, networking with industry professionals, taking calculated risks, and maintaining patience and persistence, you are well-positioned to achieve your goal of becoming a millionaire through real estate. So go out there and start building your path to success today!

Conclusion

"Millionaire by 20 from Real Estate Investment" is a groundbreaking non-fiction book that aims to help readers achieve financial success through real estate investment. The book provides practical advice and strategies based on extensive research, analysis, and insights from experts in the field.

The main topics covered in the book include understanding market trends, identifying lucrative investment opportunities, and building a successful real estate portfolio. The authors provide step-by-step guidance on various investment strategies such as flipping properties, rental income, and long-term appreciation. They also explore financing options, tax benefits, and risk management techniques to ensure profitable and sustainable investments.

One notable aspect of the book is its accessibility. The authors break down complex concepts into easy-to-understand language, making it suitable for readers of all backgrounds. The tone of the book is motivational yet practical, aiming to inspire readers with real-life examples and stories while emphasizing the dedication, discipline, and work ethic required for financial success at a young age.

The authors have conducted extensive research to gather relevant information about real estate investment trends and statistics. They have also studied successful books in this field to craft a unique resource that stands out from existing publications. By incorporating keyword research into their writing process, they ensure maximum visibility and reach for their book.

Overall, "Millionaire by 20 from Real Estate Investment" offers valuable insights into real estate investment for both novice investors and those with some experience in the field. It provides a comprehensive guide to navigating the world of real estate investment and unlocking the potential for wealth creation. If you are ready to take control of your financial future and embark on a journey towards financial freedom, this book is designed to meet your needs. Start building your path to becoming a millionaire today!

Acknowledgements

- "The Book on Rental Property Investing" by Brandon Turner

- "The Millionaire Real Estate Investor" by Gary Keller

- "Real Estate Investing For Dummies" by Eric Tyson and Robert S. Griswold

- "The ABCs of Real Estate Investing" by Ken McElroy

- "Rich Dad Poor Dad" by Robert Kiyosaki (includes real estate investment principle)

- "Keyword Research: A Definitive Guide" by Backlinko - "The Art of SEO: Mastering Search Engine Optimization" by Eric Enge, Stephan Spencer, and Jessie Stricchiola

- "Keyword Research for Search Engine Optimization: The Ultimate Guide" by Matthew Capala - "SEO 2021: Learn search engine optimization with smart internet marketing strategies" by Adam Clarke

- "The Intelligent Investor" by Benjamin Graham

- "Market Wizards" by Jack D. Schwager

- "The Little Book of Common Sense Investing" by John C. Bogle

- "A Random Walk Down Wall Street" by Burton G. Malkiel

- "The Real Estate Game" by William J. Poorvu

- "The Book on Investing in Real Estate with No (and Low) Money Down" by Brandon Turner

- "The Complete Guide to Real Estate Finance for Investment Properties" by Steve Berges

- "Real Estate Finance and Investments: Risks and Opportunities" by Peter Linneman

- "The Book on Tax Strategies for the Savvy Real Estate Investor" by Amanda Han and Matthew MacFarland

- "Real Estate Taxation: A Practitioner's Guide" by David F. Windish

- "Tax-Free Wealth: How to Build Massive Wealth by Permanently Lowering Your Taxes" by Tom Wheelwright

- "The Handbook of Real Estate Portfolio Management" by Joseph L. Pagliari Jr., Richard T. Monopoli, and James R. DeLisle

- "Real Estate Finance and Investments: Risks and Opportunities" by Peter Linneman

- "Real Estate Risk Analysis: Techniques and Tools for Measuring Risk in Real Estate Investments" by Simon Stevenson

- "Real Estate Investing For Dummies" by Eric Tyson and Robert S. Griswold

- "The 4-Hour Workweek" by Timothy Ferriss

www.ingramcontent.com/pod-product-compliance
Lightning Source LLC
Chambersburg PA
CBHW070221260726
48658CB00006BA/2130